AUTHOR

Ben Locwin
Ben Locwin is a behavioral neuroscientist and healthcare and medical executive who champions neuroscience in the learning and talent development fields. He has written several books and articles about improving employee performance in high-risk organizations. He has worked in various industries—including aerospace and automotive, food and beverage, and energy—and has collaborated with hospitals and clinical centers to improve patient outcomes.

Content Manager, Talent Management
Zaimah Khan

Editor, *TD at Work*
Patty Gaul

Managing Editor
Joy Metcalf

Graphic Designer
Shirley E.M. Raybuck

Feedback. We all have delivered it at one point or another, and everyone has certainly received it. Yet, interestingly, for something so ubiquitous, people often feel unsatisfied by the message they've conveyed or received.

Take the slippery, undefined behavioral aspects of giving feedback and layer onto it the fact that it most often occurs in organizational situations of discontent and within a kludgy software platform. This not only adds complexity and bureaucracy, but it also acts to distance the individual delivering and the individual receiving the feedback by way of an impersonal barrier.

If you've been to a doctor's office recently, this should feel familiar: As the United States' move to electronic health records has created a maelstrom of dissatisfied patients and disenfranchisement within the healthcare system, a cottage industry has popped up with books, lectures, conferences, and webinars trying to offer solutions to break down—not increase—the artificial tech barriers to receiving medical care. Technology is not always the best way to approach better communication and information transference and is often the key limiting factor. Healthcare, by its very nature, seems to people to require a personal and face-to-face discussion without distracting elements.

Why should career-trajectory-influencing feedback be any different? The reality: It's not, but there's a great degree of discomfort about it.

According to a 2016 Interact study that Harris Poll conducted, a stunning 69 percent of managers say they are uncomfortable communicating with their staff. And they aren't to blame. Managers generally don't have the credentials to give or write feedback. Most managers (more than 67 percent, according to Gallup) have had no training in performance reviews or giving feedback; further, according to ATD Research, 73 percent of new people managers don't receive training on the topic of feedback until after starting their new role.

Imagine this: If you needed some electrical work done, would you find a contractor who was a credentialed electrician or would you hire anyone who offered to do the job regardless of whether the individual had done it before? Unfortunately for most professionals, great complexity is involved in getting better performance out of people than in almost any other corporate endeavor. Further, there's an incredible void of evidence-based practices for performance reviews and feedback training.

In this TD at Work, I will discuss:
- the importance of feedback and challenges to productive feedback discussions
- why performance and feedback discussions go awry
- how to personalize feedback and performance discussions based on the recipient
- considerations for measuring the effectiveness of your performance and feedback sessions.

This issue of TD at Work will give talent development professionals the tools to assist managers in providing performance feedback more effectively. It's simple: Better feedback leads to better performance.

The Importance of Feedback

According to the U.S. Office of Personnel Management, effective feedback "is a critical component of a successful performance management program and should be used in conjunction with setting performance goals. If effective feedback is given to employees on their progress towards their goals, employee performance will improve." Feedback can come from a variety of sources—think 360-degree assessments that include input from a manager, peers, and so forth. For the purposes of this issue of TD at Work, however, I'm talking about feedback from managers. While my primary audience is talent development professionals, anyone who manages staff or endeavors to do so can use the information in this issue to help understand how to provide effective feedback.

> **The closer feedback is to the execution of an activity, the more informative and helpful it is.**

The Nobel laureate Daniel Kahneman observed that "expertise is learned from prolonged experience with good feedback on mistakes." Humans are creatures shaped by classical and operant conditioning. The closer feedback is to the execution of an activity, the more informative and helpful it is. This course correction, whether gradual and minutely incremental or broad and diametrically sweeping, is the architecture of how people learn and improve their skills at anything. They learn by course correcting.

Challenges to Great Performance Feedback

Although everyone may claim to have an unspoken agreement that feedback is good, how feedback looks and feels in practice is much different. Look at the systems stacked against managers: A manager who has five or 10 (or more) direct reports is responsible, at least once per year, for writing a review for each employee. And because organizations increasingly expect feedback on a regular basis, not just once a year, managers have a greater duty. This should make perfect sense—for feedback to be the most effective for improving performance, it needs to be contemporaneous with the observed behavior. Telling someone quarterly that his particular selling skill or email etiquette needs improvement is not only unhelpful but encourages those behaviors to persist and may have even engrained them.

As Patrick Malone and Zina B. Sutch wrote in their TD article, "The Fear of Feedback," "Whether you are the giver or receiver, feedback strikes fear into the hearts of even the most seasoned manager." Think about a situation where a manager was formerly a peer to someone who now is her direct report or a manager and direct report who are friends outside of work. On the flipside, consider a manager and direct report who don't quite see eye to eye but need to work together. The potential bias in any of these situations makes feedback and reviews more challenging. I was fortunate to have met with Doug Stone, co-author with Sheila Heen of *Thanks for the Feedback*, and was asked to write a review of it. What struck me in the book was the prominence with which trust plays a role in the feedback cycle. Building culture is an iterative process and needs to be nurtured.

Do you know where the real unity manifests around the time of annual performance reviews? It's in the coffee bars, cafeterias, and other social gathering places in a company. Here, a solidarity is built among staff as they unify against the notion of the performance management process. On average, they hate it–but it doesn't have to be this way.

For example, I gathered data from two client sites by surveying 486 participants on how they felt about their company's performance management system. On a scale of 1-7, where 7 is highly rated, the average (mean) is 2.4, and the median is 2.7. This result doesn't even approach the level of indifference, that is, the middle of the scale.

On top of these considerations, how a manager gives feedback to her direct reports varies depending on the employees' personality, as well as team dynamics overall. Let's take a closer look.

Personalizing Performance Feedback

All too often, feedback and performance reviews comprise of boilerplate, cookie-cutter feedback to the masses, which encourages disenfranchisement in the company from the get-go. Consider, instead, whether managers implemented a modern approach where different people in different functions were treated like nondiscretionary elements of a larger collective. Within different functions in an organization, employees are undertaking different types of work, and each person within a function has disparate needs. Taken as a whole, this is what creates the overall trajectory for the firm. Why, then, would companies treat each function and person the same? They shouldn't.

Instead, the most effective way to give feedback and conduct performance reviews is to focus on the behaviors that each person engages in, look at the results, and find where the individual's personal characteristics converge with the performance of the role and function. In this way, it's possible to optimize the organization as an entity instead of simply suboptimizing all employees as a faceless collective.

Changing the Negative Performance Dynamic

The basis of the model for an organization being sentient is looking at the individual employee as an individual and his role and function within the firm. In *Wall Street & Technology*, Becca Lipman writes, "In the last few years, the idea of a sentient enterprise has taken hold–a corporation whose parts are so intimately connected they are essentially a single, very powerful entity." She continues, "A sentient organization harnesses real-time capabilities, social information, applications, and artificial intelligence to advance the overall organization."

In other words: Your organization should function as a self-aware, understanding entity. That is the reason different functions exist.

In the human body, specialized organ systems do work that no other systems can do–and they are necessary as part of an interdependent whole. The same should be true in an organization. For example, you have outwardly looking business intelligence staff who function much along the lines of the body's sensory systems, sensing the competitive environment in which the company is working. These individuals return information that the larger organization can use to formulate immediate course corrections or longer-term strategic objectives. This information is often not perfect, and it's fraught with uncertainty, but on average, it allows for better decision making than not having it at all.

In the holistic systems approach to organizational performance, if individuals–as well as discrete groups–in

> ### Why Frequent Feedback Is Needed for Today's Organizations
>
> Imagine this: There's a food truck a few blocks from your office that you've heard about via word of mouth. You may decide to venture out to explore its offerings. But by the time you get there, it may already be closed. Or perhaps it has run out of certain items, changing the overall mix of choices you can make.
>
> That is similar to having imprecise business intelligence data and committing organizational resources to particular courses of action. By the time you execute on them, things may have changed. You're making choices about what the company should do at the same time that external variables are evolving. The context of what you started out doing may have changed.
>
> This is why nimbleness and agility are so important for managers—especially now more than ever, given the rate at which the external environment is changing. That is one reason annual performance reviews are no longer adequate. The skill sets required of employees, as well as the disruption that is occurring in organizations, industries, and the business world as a whole creates a greater level of flux and unpredictability, necessitating a greater level of discussion, more frequently.
>
> This can be summed up by an apropos metaphor that hockey legend Wayne Gretzky used: "I skate to where the puck is going, not where it is." By the time you execute on what is now, the now has already changed—you're essentially deciding in arrears. Managers need to have performance discussions with the future in mind.

organizations are necessarily specialized for the company's optimum benefit and architecture, why would the organization treat them all the same? Their performance looks (and should look) appreciably different, and their outputs and motivations are different. Homogenizing feedback and performance management for the employees is counterproductive and patronizing, pandering to HR systems. The revolutionary approach is to fully tailor the performance review and feedback discussions to individuals and their working conditions—not to deliver the same message the same way across the board to appear unbiased.

Start With Why

How should managers address individual review and feedback sessions in a way that gets people out of the box? They can start by identifying the *why* of each function's existence in the organization. This can be likened to author, speaker, and organizational consultant Simon Sinek's approach of "start with why"—although people and organizations have been in search of the why for thousands of years.

Managers shouldn't assume they know why a certain group of individuals (such as business analysts, HR specialists, or event planners) exists because they know the name of the function. To tailor feedback to the specific work and worker, managers should know what the critical business levers are within that function to help the overall company thrive, as well as what happens if individuals in the group don't operate successfully. This gives an indication of what the value-added work is that the people in these functions produce—and therefore, the barometer against which they should measure performance.

The Analytical Employee

If an employee works in business analytics, she—and her work—is likely more analytical. In the adjacent figure, the social analytical axis increases as you move to the top and right. The employee archetype represented by the red dot is highly analytical but perhaps less social. This individual may be the organization's guru within technical functions who is on a spectrum of more analytical and less social.

How should a manager craft and deliver feedback to someone who is more analytical or introspective? In this case, the best approach to performance discussions is to start with objective, quantified (where possible) feedback and to nurture the social aspects for personal employee development. This may look something like starting with the employee's individual performance metrics as the

The Analytical/Social Spectrum

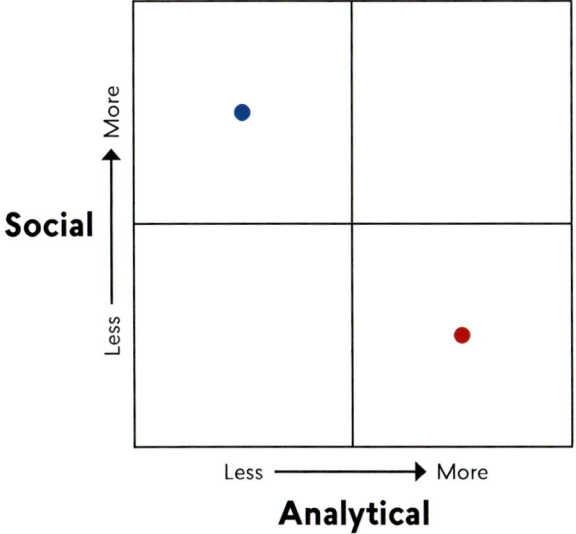

backbone of the discussion to meet her zeal for analyticity face-to-face. This doesn't mean that the manager needs to change his own personality to try to have the same level of data-analytical horsepower that this type of employee may possess and use on a daily basis in her role, but the individual will appreciate the manager's effort and feedback delivery, which will serve to be more effective in driving the conversation to new levels if the manager considers the employee's analytical tendencies.

Remember, though, that managers should nurture the individual's personal and social aspects in the discussion as well. Even for employees who are overtly shy, reserved, or lacking in a Type A energized social persona, it's a fundamental flaw not to try to balance the discussion in such a way as to help the employee both professionally and personally. That means having an open dialogue on social aspects of work, the hierarchies, and other interactive factors between colleagues that add up to being able to perform in a way that is required as part of complex human dynamics. After all, every organization comprises a diverse pool of individuals who need to collaborate for the best possible outcomes. Ignoring the social factors, even during a performance review, is a shortfall of many feedback sessions across many industries.

The Social Employee

In the same figure, the blue dot, or social employee, represents the diametric opposite of the red dot, or analytical employee: an individual who perhaps lacks analytical skills but who is high on the social factors. This could—and likely should—be an entirely different conversation from the one the manager has with the analytical employee. In this case, speaking to the heart of the employee so that he hears the message requires the manager to lead with language that is compatible with how the employee thinks and functions—that is, socially. The people-person extrovert may be an HR specialist, public relations professional, or event planner.

A feedback conversation that is likely to be more effective with this archetype would look something like this: The manager leads into the discussion about the social (and potentially largely intangible) factors that are motivating the employee, leading to his successes or failures, allowing much of a qualitative discussion to occur. However, as with the recommendation above for the analytical employee, this does not mean neglecting, in this case, the quantitative aspects of the individual's work. It could entail having nurturing discussions about how she can develop professionally by having a deeper understanding of certain technical aspects of the business or by suggesting new and novel ways to measure and refine work performance in an analytical way.

This helps balance out the persona so that, once again, the manager encourages and coaches multidimensional human beings on how to live and thrive in a dynamic work environment. In this instance, the manager may talk about how the HR specialist can improve his data analytic skills in discussions around employee engagement levels. For the public relations professional, it could include improving her understanding of email campaign response rates.

Consider two hypothetical conversations: one that you may overhear between two engineers debating the benefits of a certain material structure in designing a new prototype and the other, perhaps, between two marketing directors who are trying to design a new pitch or messaging to drive breakthrough sales to Millennials for a new product. Though both may be in the same language, the content and context of those conversations are likely disparate—different fields, competencies, backgrounds, and end goals. All these add up to produce entirely unique sets of debate. This ties back to the reason the work is different and why distinct functions need an individualized approach.

Caveat to the Personalities Discussion

The prior employee examples are not meant to suggest that individuals are limited to those characteristics. Many have been conditioned to believe this—that all analytically rigorous people are recluses or that all salespeople are quantitatively void. That is not true. The Analytical/Social Spectrum figure leaves open the other two possibilities for an individual with low analytical rigor and low social aspects and a person with high analytical rigor and high social aspects. Don't fall prey to cognitive myths that possessing one type of trait makes it likely or inevitable that an individual will be devoid of another type of trait. Just as learning styles (such as kinesthetic, visual, or auditory) are a myth, so too are these preconceptions.

This is where it's important for managers to get to know their direct reports to more fully understand them and their personalities. Doing so will greatly improve the feedback conversations and, thus, performance. But how do they do this?

How to Provide Feedback Well

Amee Patel Pant, organizational consultant and founder of an HR consulting group, explains that managers are responsibile for understanding that there are multiple personalities in their department and that they need to adapt (but not cater—there's a difference) to each individual. Managers should take into consideration the employee they are reviewing: How does this person receive and react to feedback? What could be causing her performance to exceed expectations or, on the flipside, be an area where she needs to improve? How is she motivated—for example, does she prefer public or private recognition? What are her career advancement goals? Is she in search of stability or change and adventure?

Management is a discipline, and so it happens daily, not after one day. For this reason, managers should continuously sharpen their proverbial saw and frequently check in with employees—that beats irregular, random pronouncements every time.

> **It's important for managers to get to know their direct reports to more fully understand them and their personalities. Doing so will greatly improve the feedback conversations and, thus, performance.**

Patel Pant notes that, at some point, it isn't just about the written documentation, which has long been the case for performance reviews. It is about the managers and the way in which they deliver the appraisal. Are they giving sincere constructive feedback while also making the employee feel valued and motivated to work smarter and better? Or are they giving the critical feedback with the employee walking out feeling disheartened and disengaged?

Tailoring Discussions to Your Audience

Leadership and coaching expert John Maxwell captured the notion exceptionally well in his book *The 21 Irrefutable Laws of Leadership* that just having great talent in one's organization isn't enough. It's important to know what drives them and how to motivate them. He recounts a story of football coach Lou Holtz, who said, "You can't win without good athletes, but you can lose with them. This is where coaching makes the difference." This means that just having top talent, technical or otherwise, isn't a guarantee of performance or success—and those two words are not synonyms. You can perform but not achieve success.

Encouraging the best out of top talent requires careful assessment and tailoring of your performance management practices and feedback approaches. If the smartest, most talented individuals were apt to spontaneously self-assemble into high-performing teams, startup companies would pop up in universities and coffee shops daily and have 100 percent success rates. They wouldn't be special anymore because startups would launch all the time. This doesn't happen. That's why managers and conversations around developing their direct reports are so important.

According to *Thanks for the Feedback*, if the recipient of your feedback thinks it's incorrect, the individual won't listen. Your relationship with the individual—not just the content—matters.

When you're coaching or giving feedback, you're creating and participating in a dynamic. A dynamic takes two (or more) entities, so it doesn't just matter what you think and feel and imagine you're conveying as the manager; it also matters how the recipient receives your feedback.

Trust Is the Core of Feedback

Providing feedback well is based on trust. Teams that have psychological safety and trust have higher performance outcomes and fewer incidences of self-sabotage. Taking this a bit further, it's the people elements of work—the knowledge, skills, reputations, and relationships—that work together to generate the highest business value.

Just like many HR functions have rebranded themselves as people operations or some similar moniker that brings *people* to the forefront, the individuals with whom you share feedback are people. Organizations try to bureaucratize the language to make it sound more sterile and less human. But note the irony here: Any company that says, "People are our greatest asset" and then circulates emails referring to people as "reqs," "heads," and so forth is being hypocritical.

As Patel Pant sums up, managers can help build trust by taking the time to prepare and thoughtfully think about how to give feedback in different ways to individuals with varying personalities. It will show direct reports that managers care about their development. Most important, managers shouldn't think of it as another annoying HR process but as a way to make behavioral adjustments to ensure organizational success and future career success.

Appreciation

Appreciation is critical. Managers should be encouraged to give more. The negative feedback is always an emergency, but the positive feedback moments apparently never are.

Performance Feedback for Younger Workers

While the fast-pace of business is one reason performance feedback needs to occur more frequently than once a year, young workers also expect regular feedback sessions.

Tom Gimbel, founder and CEO at LaSalle Network—a recruiting, staffing, and culture firm—wrote in his *Fortune* article "Why Your Younger Employees Hate Performance Reviews" that "Where a lot of companies fail is trying to offer millennials 'success,' but without speaking their language." He notes that Millennials want to feel challenged and part of the company mission and aspire to make a difference. Further, if you wait a year, you're likely to lose many of those younger workers.

A 2015 Trinet survey echoed Gimbel's sentiments, reporting that Millennials are fighting back against inadequate performance reviews in several ways. The HR service provider found that 28 percent of Millennials looked for a new job because of an unsatisfactory performance review process; 35 percent have complained to co-workers; and 15 percent cursed and cried.

The survey noted that Millennial respondents want more frequent feedback—85 percent said they'd feel more confident in their position with more frequent conversations. Those conversations should include specific feedback, consist of an open dialogue, and be fair and unbiased.

And while performance discussions should be frequent, Millennials never want them to be a surprise. If your direct reports feel blindsided by performance reviews, that's an ambush—not good management. Have more frequent discussions with Millennial and Generation Z workers, and give them advance notice.

As managers come to know their direct reports as individuals, they'll come to understand how these individuals like to be acknowledged. Whether it's an email, thank-you note, or public acknowledgement at a weekly team meeting–do it. Remember, the individual employees within an organization aren't colored dots as in the Analytical/Social Spectrum figure; however, that example serves to illustrate that individuals are exactly that: individual. As talent development professionals, we can ensure that they are receiving the feedback, recognition, and critique they need, when they need it, in a way that best connects to their underlying cognitive preference.

There's a lot within business and organizations that is more probability and randomness than we'd like to believe. This doesn't mean throwing up our hands and just letting it ride because it's random. Rather, it means that individuals' ability to identify key roles and key players, monitor performance, and give good feedback can adjust the future state compared with an alternative scenario of not doing these things properly.

Feedback and Monetary Value

What about pay? How about promotions? Those are other aspects that come up frequently. Employees have come to assume that feedback sessions are either complaint sessions or an opportunity to jockey for titles and pay raises. If managers are holding performance discussions infrequently, then, sure, the performance reviews may annually coincide with an employee looking for a merit increase or a promotion. But they shouldn't be explicitly tied to promotions or raises.

The reason is a bit complex; the field of behavioral economics has identified ample nuance as to how individuals think about incentives. It's not always–and really, almost never is–just about money. In fact, in many experimental conditions where people are given opportunities to work for certain perks and rewards, the nonmonetary rewards produce better output from the individuals. If an organization or team is tying reviews to money, it needs to stop. More frequent feedback sessions and performance discussions can begin to decouple them from dollar signs. When managers help shape performance, they incentivize employees in several ways.

American psychologist Frederick Herzberg was one of the first to research and document the reasons employees are motivated to work. What he found was that pay is usually somewhere around third place as far as what keeps employees motivated to perform and to work better–not harder, because you want employees to produce better results, not just more of the same results. Recognition is the goal, and, no, that doesn't need to mean ice cream socials or other ineffective nonsense. Having managers and leaders frequently check the company's pulse and give recognitive feedback to employees to show that they're valued is all that's required. It's simple yet simply underdone. The U.S. Department of Labor reports that more than 90 percent of American workers feel underappreciated at work. Of the people who voluntarily leave their jobs, about 50 percent say it's due to lack of appreciation.

Don't Shy Away From Missed Goals

In "The Validity and Utility of Selection Methods in Personnel Psychology: Practical and Theoretical Implications of 85 Years of Research Findings," Frank Schmidt and John Hunter suggest that job-specific, structured interview and discussion topics are better predictors of job performance compared to unstructured questions. Additionally, bringing failures (or missed goals) into your organization's discussions more often is an excellent and profound way to encourage performance improvement.

Not everything is going to go perfectly. Not every goal is going to have been scoped well (or even properly), but when problems and failures become more of a comfortable discussion point, the organization can begin to identify the systemic factors that can improve many of the facets that seem to continually generate nonconformances. Further, the changing world of business means necessary changes to goals and what positive performance looks like.

Avoid Micromanagement

Micromanagement isn't conducive to better performance management or feedback. At Google, one of nine behavioral measures of a manager is that "They do not micromanage by getting involved in details that should be handled at other levels." Micromanagement does not beget good feedback, it's not good management, and it doesn't help the organization with anything except motivating top performers to leave the building.

What If I Like (or Don't Like) an Employee?

As a manager, just saying you like the people who are your direct reports isn't enough for a sustainable culture, nor for effective business performance. But it is important to have high likeability across and within functions. It makes people's days more enjoyable during the long hours that they're working together, and it factors in to a high degree within the collaboration dimension of team performance.

However, beware. In research on quick assessments of managers' likeability and performance that Benny Geys presents in *The Leadership Quarterly*, the "likeability aversion" is when employees prefer to a lesser extent managers with higher perceived likeability than managers with lower perceived likeability. Interestingly, this effect is highly durable and appears in male and female respondents, affects male and female managers, and was reported from employee groups as well as HR departments.

Consider this example (names are changed to protect the individuals): Mary is a vice president of customer service who manages Katie, a customer service manager. Mary and Katie are friendly outside the office. Katie is responsible for a customer-service-level agreement that has been slipping every quarter. Mary has attempted to bring up the dropping key performance indicator but often beats around the bush because she doesn't want to create hard feelings. It does not help that Mary is aware that Katie is sensitive to negative feedback.

Instead of providing the clear and honest feedback that will greatly help Katie grow professionally and cease hurting the organization, Mary gives Katie glowing reviews and writes about Katie's successes in her position. Soon, other managers see the decline in customer service KPIs and Katie loses credibility with her peers and the senior managers. The lack of performance feedback hurts everyone involved: Katie, Mary, and the organization.

It's the Human Dynamic

Although HR professionals think that having a software platform to track and trend all the annual performance review data adds validity and gravitas to the activities, it doesn't. A paper-based system works just as well, because it's all about the value of the conversations. Industry data show that more than 90 percent (and in some circles, more than 99.4 percent) of companies use software tools and platforms, and they give HR personnel a false sense of security. It's not about tracking and trending—especially of qualitative information. It's about the recognitive value of the human-to-human interactions.

What Do You Evaluate?

Should a manager offer feedback and evaluate only on a direct report's SMART (specific, measurable, achievable, relevant, and time-bound) goals? I receive that question often, and the answer is that I hope not. Certainly, arranging work via SMART goals (or any other acronymized goals) can provide individuals with the ability to assess discrete feedback points. But there's more to performance than that. First, let's remember the individuals and their functions, two huge components and sources of variation in the feedback equation. Beyond that, Patel Pant says that performance appraisals have a powerful role in helping to ensure that the employee is working toward established goals that benefit the organization and toward self-improvement and career progression. It is also a great opportunity to hear about the employee's career goals and is useful in aligning business objectives in a way that furthers the individual's professional growth.

In addition to greater development for the individual and how it ties with business objectives, performance discussions offer a great opportunity to review the bigger picture about the organizational mission and direction. Google's mission statement has been touted as: "to organize the world's information and make it universally accessible and useful." As Laszlo Bock, co-founder and CEO of Humu and formerly the senior vice president of people operations at Google, observed correctly, "This is a moral goal, not a business one."

Are You Energizing Employees?

Feedback conversations, from a purely HR metrics perspective, are about driving some fundamental movement around how employees work and change within organizations. Some of the contemporary metrics around this include retention, attrition rate, and regrettable turnover. But here's a secret: Each of these metrics is fundamentally flawed, easily (and usually) gamed, and often unhelpful. Instead, you need to be energizing your employees.

Think about your people operations' metrics, such as the three I mentioned and ask yourself how easily you've correlated your HR data with things that you can't, or couldn't, possibly influence. You may want to think that a new HR initiative that launched two months ago is the reason retention has seemed to stabilize or improve over that time period. Unfortunately, you're not accounting for the other reasons, including seasonality, a new snack offering, or any number of factors.

Similarly, with attrition rate, when it gets bad, I've seen many companies—including large, successful ones—blame it on everything external from HR to the business operations; yet, when it becomes more favorable, the companies are quick to take all the credit.

Don't overlook regrettable turnover, or the departure of employees the company wanted to retain. Every employee should be an individual you want to retain—if not, you haven't done a good job with feedback sessions and performance management. You should have gotten rid of the underperformers a long time ago so that any current losses are, indeed, regrettable.

People want to be challenged and grow professionally in an organization; they are not just there for the paycheck. Ask yourself whether you have left your employees energized and excited about their future working with you and the organization.

Most importantly, don't let C players linger in the organization—it will cause resentment for their coworkers. Further, you are not helping the organization reach its full potential by doing so. One of my favorite quotes is from Narayana Murthy, Infosys founder: "You have to hire A players. If you hire B players, they will hire C players, and the C players will hire D players, and pretty soon you have a bunch of idiots running the company."

If you mistakenly hired wrong, use the performance review to demonstrate the potential of your direct reports to become A players. It is your duty as a manager. Take the time to prepare and thoughtfully think about how to give feedback in different ways to the different personalities you have on your team and in the organization. Don't think of it as another annoying HR process but as a way to make behavioral adjustments to ensure organizational, and future career, success.

The vision statement helps the culture to arrange itself according to a set of fundamental principles. The lofty statement is impossible to achieve and was written intentionally so. It keeps Google and its employees ever-developing and pushing the envelope. It also makes feedback and performance management a more fluid situation. For an organization striving to make the world's information universally accessible and useful—something that is impossible—performance feedback may revolve, at least in part, not on attaining that goal but being earnest, creative, and energized by constant striving.

Remember: Feedback, when done well, drives better performance. But organizations don't exist for the sole purpose of creating activity and generating feedback. Feedback should be thought of as a supportive tool that helps the organization be more effective at realizing its mission statement and returning value for its customers and shareholders.

In his ATD webcast, "5 Keys to Effective Feedback to Drive Performance," Ike Bennion of Instructure explained that performance isn't just based on what you do but also on how you do it and how you do so with other people. The *what* concerns areas of responsibilities, with the *how* considering competencies such as open communication and organizational skills; meanwhile, how you do it with others concerns organizational citizenship, such as helping to foster trust among co-workers.

Further, in "What Is Performance Feedback?" Kimberlee Leonard suggests adding quality of work, work habits, service habits, and team skills as potential areas for feedback. A manager may not acknowledge a customer representative, for example, simply for answering a client's question. Rather, her manager may offer positive feedback because she asked the customer questions to let him know that she was listening to him. Or the manager may recognize her direct report because she offered to cover customer hours for a colleague on vacation or over a holiday.

W. Edwards Deming mused, "It is not enough to do your best; you must know what to do, and then do your best." Knowing what to do and getting feedback on how to do it well (or better) is what will drive a high-performance organization.

Systems Approach: Group Behavior

If I draw upon my earlier idea of the holistic workplace and every function working together to produce the whole, it becomes incumbent upon me to address group dynamics. When I advise organizations about the psychological dynamics of group behavior, I try to stress that when talent development professionals work with, or consider, individuals, it elicits a personal (that is, human) response. When we participate in large groups or look at an impersonal Excel list of full-time equivalents—for example, when an organization is going through restructuring—or talk to a full room, we tend not to perceive or empathize with individuals and instead perceive it as a collective. That can have profound psychological consequences, as well as resultant consequences on how we treat people.

So, as we work with diverse functions and diversity of individuals within functions, we have many layers of complexity that manifest. Try to imagine, for instance, how one feedback discussion with an individual in your organization done well can have a positive effect that reverberates through the company. The individual may work or emote differently to colleagues about his experiences, which then can virtuously affect larger and larger segments of the organization. Holding effective feedback and performance management sessions and iterating frequently across the company can be one of the most effective campaigns you can ever run to modify the business's overall performance in a positive direction.

Conclusion

Performance reviews, performance management, and feedback are all components of a well-run organization. The word *organization* comes from the Latin *organum*, but its first known use as a collective of individuals as we use it today appears to have first occurred around 1873. Think of all the work that's been done in history to get the work world to the place it is at right now. Only in about the past century and a half have organizations been considered in some of the ways that they are now. As society gets more and more refined in its thinking and work, talent development professionals need to also evolve and bring employees to the next level of what we expect from them in terms of performance and production. To do anything less is a disservice to ourselves, our employees, and our customers—whatever product or service it is that we're developing for them.

We work for various personal reasons, as well as our collective societal reasons. And through it all, we're people. Working with human dynamics requires more than just a blunt instrument. Getting more and more precise work accomplished more effectively requires that we also bring along the next generation of employees to do that good work. The tips and recommendations in this issue of *TD at Work* were designed specifically to give you new ways of thinking about how work gets done, how work should get done, and how to identify that gray space in between those two phrases and areas.

We get better work outputs every time we recognize and can name the issues that currently exist and then work to improve them. Many of the fundamental stalling and inflection points within organizations owe their loci to human dynamics. We can't get around the cultural aspects of work; nor should we want to. We should endeavor to address and solve the best ways of going about working with people. That alone can bring your business to new echelons of performance. It's not easy. But it's simple.

References & Resources

Books

Bock, L. 2015. *Work Rules! Insights from Inside Google That Will Transform How You Live and Lead.* New York, NY: Hachette Book Group.

Herzberg, F., B. Mausner, and B.B. Snyderman. 1959. *The Motivation to Work.* 2nd ed. Oxford, England: John Wiley.

Maxwell, J. 2007. *The 21 Irrefutable Laws of Leadership: Follow Them and People Will Follow You.* Nashville, TN: Thomas Nelson.

Schmidt, E., and J. Rosenberg. 2017. *How Google Works.* New York, NY: Grand Central Publishing.

Sinek, S. 2011. *Start with Why: How Great Leaders Inspire Everyone to Take Action.* New York, NY: Penguin Group.

Stone, D., and S. Heen. 2015. *Thanks for the Feedback: The Science and Art of Receiving Feedback Well.* New York, NY: Penguin Random House.

Online Resources

ACTPS Government. n.d. "The Art of Feedback: Giving, Seeking and Receiving Feedback." www.cmtedd.act.gov.au/__data/assets/pdf_file/0003/463728/art_feedback.pdf.

ATD. n.d. "5 Keys of Effective Feedback to Drive Performance." www.td.org/videos/5-keys-of-effective-feedback-to-drive-performance.

ATD. 2019. *Developing New Managers.* March. www.td.org/research-reports/developing-new-managers.

Baldoni, J. 2015. "A-C-T: 3 Tips for Receiving Feedback." ATD Insights, January 22. www.td.org/insights/a-c-t-3-tips-for-receiving-feedback.

Geys, B. 2014. "Better Not Look Too Nice? Employees' Preferences Towards (Un)Likeable Managers." *The Leadership Quarterly* 25(5): 875-884.

Gimbel, T. 2017. "Why Your Younger Employees Hate Performance Reviews." *Fortune*, February 13. http://fortune.com/2017/02/13/millennial-employees-performance-reviews.

Interact. 2016. "Many Leaders Shrink from Straight Talk with Employees." February. http://interactauthentically.com/articles/research/many-leaders-shrink-straight-talk-employees.

Leonard, K. 2018. "What Is Performance Feedback?" Chron, August 20. https://smallbusiness.chron.com/performance-feedback-1882.html.

Schmidt, F.L., and J.E. Hunter. 1998. "The Validity and Utility of Selection Methods in Personnel Psychology: Practical and Theoretical Implications of 85 Years of Research Findings." *Psychological Bulletin* 124(2): 262-274. https://scinapse.io/papers/2136971664.

Trinet. 2015. "Survey: Performance Reviews Drive One in Four Millennials to Search for a New Job or Call in Sick." www.trinet.com/about-us/news-press/press-releases/survey-performance-reviews-drive-one-in-four-millennials-to-search-for-a-new-job-or-call-in-sick.

U.S. Office of Personnel Management. n.d. "Performance Management Performance Management Cycle: Feedback is Critical to Improving Performance." www.opm.gov/policy-data-oversight/performance-management/performance-management-cycle/monitoring/feedback-is-critical-to-improving-performance.

Yaya, P. 2018. "Your Weekly Top 5: How to Receive Feedback Effectively." On the Job, January 26. https://blogs.agu.org/onthejob/2018/01/26/weekly-top-5-receive-feedback-effectively.

Job Aid

Feedback Conversation Preparation Template

Managers can use this guidance and the form template to prepare for feedback conversations with direct reports.

Prepare the Space
Just as in your personal space, having an appropriate, quiet, neat space to conduct conversations is the best way to have feedback discussions. No distractions due to noise, clutter, phone alerts, and so forth.

Be Ready
Have your notes ready and be ready to diverge from them.
- Include good, bad, and neutral feedback points.
- Keep it fair—for the direct report and for you.
- Don't stick to a script; use it as a guide.
- Do your homework to determine where your employee could develop within her role or within the organization; you may like the employee and think she is doing a great job, but the best thing for her and the business could be to have her take on a temporary work stint or assignment in another function, area, or region.

Deliver
Provide the hard message the way you would want to hear it: directly, without emotion, and accurately.

Provide recognition and be prepared to offer this recognition much more often, simply as a course of business. That is one of the best ways to keep employees motivated and engaged—don't just do it once or twice per year because you have to.

Take notes during the conversations. This should include:
- what your employee says, the individual's emotional reaction, and the impact you feel the conversation is having on the employee.
- what you're thinking about as you hold the discussion; use this to extend a meaningful dialogue or to build on in the next session.

Let your employee know the "and then what?" trajectory: What's next for the individual?

This is a time not to overreach. Instead, use the information you prepared in advance to help your employee grow.

Job Aid

Feedback Conversation Preparation Template (Cont.)

Use this form to prepare for your next conversation with your direct report.

Where will you have the conversation with your direct report? _____

_____

What feedback do you want to present to your direct report?

- Good _____

    _____

- Bad _____

    _____

- Neutral _____

    _____

Review your list. Is it fair?

What is the hard message you want to deliver? _____

_____

_____

Can you deliver this message based on fact and without emotion? Practice if you need to, especially as you first begin to deliver feedback.

What have you noticed about your direct report that the individual does well? _____

_____

When are the opportunities you have to deliver that recognition (such as a weekly team meeting or shared kitchen space where you cross paths)?

_____

_____

Notes from conversation: _____

_____

_____

THE SEVEN CENTRAL THEMES OF MODERN COMPLIANCE

In the modern organization, compliance training is typically implemented to manage risk in seven core areas of organizational accountability:

- **CONSUMER PROTECTIONS**
- **CIVILITY AND DIVERSITY**
- **FRAUD AND CORRUPTION**
- **ETHICS AND INTEGRITY**
- **EMPLOYEE PROTECTIONS**
- **RESPONSIBLE STEWARDSHIP**
- **DATA PRIVACY AND CYBER SECURITY**

Learn how to improve your compliance training across these seven areas in *Fully Compliant* by Travis Waugh. To find out more, visit www.td.org/books/fully-compliant.

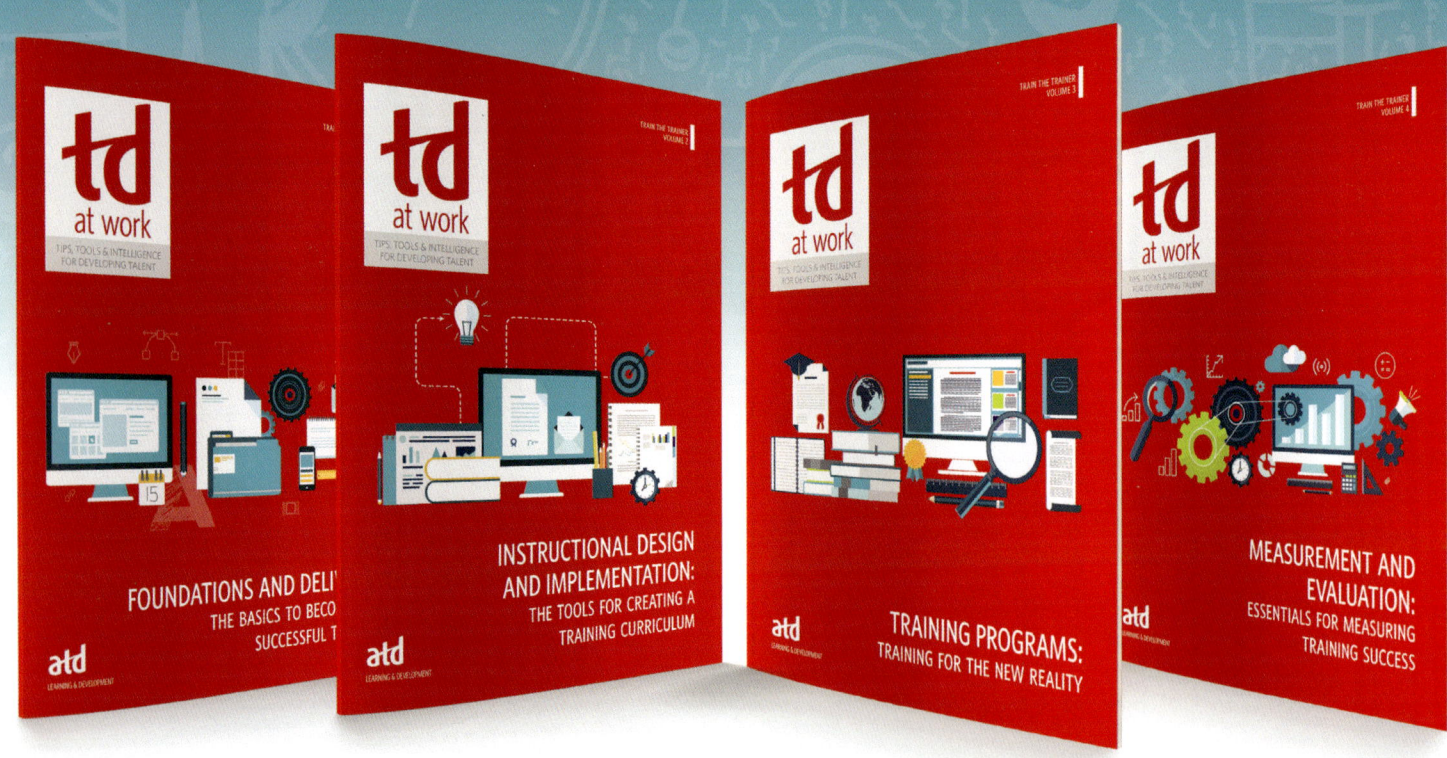